Contents

Meets Accreditation Standard for Child-created Bulletin Boards

Three Cheers for April PreK–K, SV 9841-8

Introduction

This series of monthly activity books is designed to give PreK and Kindergarten teachers a collection of hands-on activities and ideas for each month of the year. The activities are standards-based and reflect the philosophy that children learn best through play. The teacher can use these ideas to enhance the development of language and math skills, and of social/emotional and physical growth of children. The opportunity to promote pre-reading skills is present throughout the series and should be incorporated whenever possible.

Organization and Features

Each book consists of seven units:

Unit 1 provides reproducible pages and information for the month in general.
- a newsletter outline to promote parent communication
- a blank thematic border page
- a list of special days in the month
- calendar ideas to promote math skills
- a blank calendar grid that can also be used as an incentive chart

Units 2–6 include an array of activities for five **theme** topics. Each unit includes
- teacher information on the theme
- arts and crafts ideas
- a food activity
- poetry, songs, and books
- bulletin board ideas
- center activities correlated to specific learning standards

Implement the activities in a way that best meets the needs of individual children.

Unit 7 focuses on a well-known **children's author**. The unit includes
- a biography of the author
- activities based on a literature selection
- a list of books by the author
- reproducible bookmarks

In addition, each book contains
- reproducible **icons** suitable to use as labels for centers in the classroom. The icons coordinate with the centers in the book. They may also be used with a work assignment chart to aid in assigning children to centers.
- reproducible **student awards**
- **calendar day pattern** with suggested activities

Research Base

Howard Gardner's theory of multiple intelligences, or learning styles, validates teaching thematically and using a variety of approaches to help children learn. Providing a variety of experiences will assure that each child has an opportunity to learn in a comfortable way.

Following are the learning styles identified by Howard Gardner.
- **Verbal/Linguistic** learners need opportunities to read, listen, write, learn new words, and to tell stories.
- **Musical** learners enjoy music activities.
- **Logical/Mathematical** learners need opportunities to problem solve, count, measure, and do patterning activities.
- **Visual/Spatial** learners need opportunities to paint, draw, sculpt, and create art works.
- **Interpersonal** learners benefit from group discussions and group projects.
- **Intrapersonal** learners learn best in solitary activities, such as reading, writing in journals, and reflecting on information.
- **Naturalist** learners need opportunities to observe weather and nature and to take care of animals and plants.
- **Existential** learners can be fostered in the early years by asking children to think and respond, by discussions, and journal writing.

Gardner, H. (1994). *Frames of mind.* New York: Basic Books.

April News

Teacher: _____ Date: _____

Headline News

Coming Up

Happy Birthday to

Special Thanks to

Help Wanted

Three Cheers for April PreK–K, SV 9841-8

April

Unit 1, Teacher Resources: Border Page

Three Cheers for April PreK–K, SV 9841-8

Special Days in April

National Garden Month
Have children celebrate with activities from the Gardens unit that begins on page 25.

Keep America Beautiful Month Have children celebrate with activities from the Our Earth unit that begins on page 55.

National Poetry Month Read poems throughout the month and help children find the words that rhyme.

National Humor Month Discuss what humor is and read a book filled with jokes and riddles.

1 April Fools Day Read *Arthur's April Fool* by Marc Brown, or another book that focuses on this day, to the children.

2 National Peanut Butter and Jelly Day Invite children to dictate a recipe telling how to make a peanut butter and jelly sandwich. Then have them draw a picture of the sandwich.

10 Golfers Day Bring several old golf clubs and large, hollow plastic balls to school. Invite children to play golf outside during play time.

12 Look Up at the Sky Day Take the children outside and invite them to look at the sky. (Instruct them that looking at the sun is dangerous and should be avoided.) Ask them to name the things they see. If clouds are visible, have children identify shapes they see.

14 National Pecan Day Bring unshelled pecans and nutcrackers to school. Place them in a sensory tub. Challenge children to crack the nuts during center time.

18 International Jugglers Day Put scarves in the dramatic play center and challenge children to juggle two or more scarves.

22 National Jellybean Day Fill a baby food jar with jellybeans and put it in the math center. Challenge children to estimate how many candies are in the jar. Have children write their guesses on a slip of paper. At the end of the day, count the jellybeans and identify the children who guessed correctly. Then enjoy a jellybean snack.

24 National Pigs in a Blanket Day Have children wrap a hot dog in a biscuit. Bake the food according to the directions on the biscuit wrapper. As children eat the snack, discuss how the food got its name.

26 National Pretzel Day Bring two kinds of pretzels to school. Pour them into a large bowl. Invite children to take a handful. Help children make a simple graph and chart the number of each kind of pretzel they have in their hands before eating the snack.

30 Arbor Day If possible, take the children outside to sit under a tree. Explain that *arbor* comes from an old word that means "tree." Lead children in a discussion about how trees help clean the air, give shade, and give shelter. Tell children that many people like to plant trees on Arbor Day. Then read aloud *The Giving Tree* by Shel Silverstein.

Three Cheers for April PreK–K, SV 9841-8

April

Sunday	Monday	Tuesday	Wednesday	Thursday	Friday	Saturday

Unit 1, Teacher Resources: April Calendar
Three Cheers for April PreK–K, SV 9841-8

Calendar Activities for April

Classroom Calendar Setup

The use of the calendar in the classroom can provide children with daily practice on learning days, weeks, months, and years. As you plan the setup for your classroom, include enough space on the wall to staple a calendar grid labeled with the days of the week. Leave space above the grid for the name of the month and the year. Next to the calendar, staple twelve cards labeled with the months of the year and the number of days in each month. Leave these items on the wall all year. At the beginning of each month, start with the blank calendar grid. Do not staple anything on the grid that refers to the new month. Leave the days of the week and the year in place.

Introducing the Month of April

Before children arrive, gather all of the items that will go on the calendar for April. You may want to include the following:

- name of the month
- number cards
- name cards to indicate birthdays during the month
- picture cards that tell about special holidays or school events during the month
- a small treat to be taped on the day of each child's birthday. You may wish to gift wrap the treat.

Add a special pointer that can be used each day while doing calendar activities. See page 9 for directions on how to make a pointer. Place these items in a picnic basket. Select a puppet that can remain in the basket and come out only to bring items for each new month. A dog puppet works well because of the large mouth which makes it easier to grasp each item.

On the first school day of the month, follow this procedure:

1. Place the picnic basket in front of the class. Pull out the puppet and introduce it to children if it is the first time they have seen it or ask them if they remember why the puppet is here. If this is the first time they have seen it, explain that the puppet will visit on the first day of each month to bring the new calendar items.

2. Have the puppet pull out the name of the month. According to the abilities of children, have them name the first letter in the name of the month, count the letters, or find the vowels. Staple the name of the month above the calendar.

3. Have the puppet pull out the new pointer for the teacher or the daily helper to use each day during calendar time.

4. Next, pull out the number cards for April. You may use plain number cards, cards made from the calendar day pattern on page 96, or seasonal die-cut shapes. By using two or three die-cut shapes, you can incorporate building patterns as part of your daily calendar routine. See page 9 for pattern ideas.

5. Place the number one card or die-cut under the day of the week on which April begins. Locate April on the month cards that are stapled next to your calendar. Have children tell how many days this month will have and then

count that many spaces on the calendar to indicate the end of the month. You may wish to place a small stop sign as a visual reminder of the end of the month. Save the remaining numbers cards or die-cut shapes and add one each day.

6. If there are any birthdays during April, have the puppet pull out of the basket the cards that have a birthday symbol with the child's name and birth date written on it. Count from the number 1 to find where to staple this as a visual reminder of each child's birthday. If you have included a wrapped treat for each child, tape it on the calendar on the correct day.

7. Finally, have the puppet bring out cards that have pictures of holidays or special happenings, such as field trips, picture day, or story time in the library. Staple the picture cards on the correct day on the calendar grid. You can use these to practice various counting skills such as counting how many days until a field trip, a birthday, or a holiday.

8. When the basket is empty, say goodbye to the puppet and return it to the picnic basket. Put the basket away until the next month. Children will look forward to the beginning of each month in order to see what items the puppet will bring for the class calendar.

Making a Rabbit Pointer

Include a rabbit pointer in the calendar basket for this month. To make a pointer, you will need the following:

- two 3" rabbit shapes cut from poster board
- a medium-sized dowel rod that is 18" long
- several 12" lengths of narrow green and yellow ribbons

Directions

1. Hot-glue the ribbons to the end of the dowel rod so that they lie against the rod.

2. Hot-glue the two rabbit shapes to the end of the dowel rod so that the rabbits cover the glued ends of the ribbons.

The calendar helper can use this to point to the day of the week, the number, the month, and the year as the class says the date each day.

Developing a Pattern

Practice patterning by writing the numbers 1–30 on three die-cut shapes. You may want to use a raindrop, an umbrella, and a cloud. Write the numbers on the shapes in order using an ABCABCABC pattern. After the pattern has been repeated several times on the calendar, challenge children to think of other ways to make the same pattern. For example, the children might write numbers to replace the raindrop, umbrella, and cloud to make a 123123123 pattern.

Spring Talk

April comes from the word *aperio*, which means "to open." The word reflects that it is the time of year in which buds begin to grow and open.

The spring season officially begins when the sun crosses the equator, a time known as the vernal equinox. This actually happens between the dates of March 21–23. There are equal time periods of night and day.

Many ancient civilizations viewed spring as a time of renewal and rebirth. New projects that were conceived in the long, cold winter months were now started.

People in India celebrate spring by blowing dry paint on each other or squirting each other with water guns. They also use paint to make handprints on each other's backs. It is all washable, though!

April 1 is known as April Fools' Day, a day when people play jokes and pranks on each other. This tradition started in France after the change to the Gregorian calendar in 1582. Those people who did not want to accept the new calendar or who were unaware of the change got invited to places that did not exist or were given funny gifts.

The symbols of the egg and rabbit became very important. The egg was a symbol of new beginnings and life. The rabbit was a sign of growth.

Hibernating animals come out of their winter dens in spring. Scientists believe that the increase in the amount of light is the trigger that wakes the animals.

Plants start to bloom because light and warmth cause sap to begin to flow through the stem of the plant.

People in Thailand enjoy watching parades that feature a huge Buddha that squirts everyone with water. If there are no parades, people squirt each other with water.

Kites were invented in China over 3,000 years ago. The first kites were made with a bamboo frame and a silk cover.

Umbrellas were invented over 4,000 years ago. Ancient art from Egypt shows that umbrellas were used for protection from the sun. The Chinese were the first to use the umbrellas for protection from the rain. The Chinese put wax and lacquer on their colorful paper umbrellas to protect them from water.

Spring Windsock

Materials

- short cardboard tubes
- yarn
- construction paper in spring colors
- spring stickers
- tissue paper
- markers
- hole punch
- glue
- tape
- scissors

Directions

Teacher Preparation: Cut small geometric shapes out of the construction paper. Cut the tissue paper into one-half-inch wide strips. Punch three holes on one end of each tube.

1. Decorate a tube with shapes, stickers, and marker drawings.
2. Thread a long piece of yarn through all three holes.
3. Pull the yarn together in three places and tape together for a handle.
4. Tape tissue paper strips inside the bottom of the tube.
5. Fly the windsock on a windy day.

First Spring Flowers

Materials

- popped popcorn
- unpopped popcorn
- dry tempera paint
- brown tempera paint
- straws
- white construction paper
- 13-inch x 9-inch metal cake pan
- eyedropper
- resealable plastic bags
- glue

Directions

Teacher Preparation: Review the "Spring Is in Bloom" activity on page 16. After choosing the flowers to put in the center, color the popcorn the same color as the blossoms. Do this by pouring a small amount of dry tempera paint in a plastic bag, adding the popcorn, and shaking the sealed bag. Once the popcorn is colored, scoop it out and store it in another bag.

1. Place the construction paper in the pan.
2. Drop brown paint from the dropper onto the paper.
3. Using a straw, blow the paint into thin lines to make the branches.
4. Glue colored popped and unpopped popcorn on the branches to make the flowers.

11

Biscuit Umbrellas and Jelly Rain

You will need

- biscuit dough
- apple jelly
- baking tray
- paper plates
- plastic knives
- plastic spoons
- oven

Directions

1. Cut the dough for one biscuit in half.

2. Roll one half of the biscuit dough to look like a snake.

3. Make an umbrella handle out of the snake and join it to the cut side of the remaining biscuit.

4. Put the "umbrella" on a tray and bake it according to the directions on the biscuit package.

5. When cool, put the umbrella on a plate.

6. Spoon dots of jelly on and around the umbrella to make rain.

Note: Be aware of children who may have food allergies.

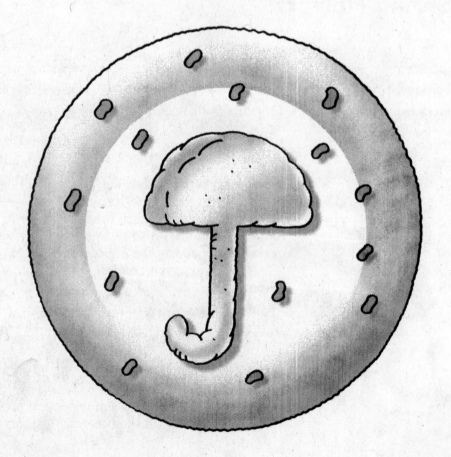

Three Cheers for April PreK–K, SV 9841-8

Bunnies in the Mud

Five little bunnies went out to play,

After a rain shower one spring day.

They squished, and they splashed, and they had such fun,

As they played in a puddle filled up with mud.

One little bunny was covered in dirt,

S/he ran home to wash her/his shirt.

Four little bunnies went out to play . . .

Three little bunnies went out to play . . .

Two little bunnies went out to play . . .

One little bunny went out to play . . .

No little bunnies went out to play,

After a rain shower one spring day.

Now that the bunnies had washed their shirts,

The sink in the house was filled with dirt.

They squished, and they splashed, and they had such fun,

As they played in a sink filled up with mud.

Spring into Some Books

Henry and Mudge in Puddle Trouble
by Cynthia Rylant (Aladdin Paperbacks)

Hopper Hunts for Spring
by Marcus Pfister (North South Books)

Mud
by Mary Lyn Ray (Harcourt)

Signs of Spring
by Justine Fontes (Mondo Pub)

Spring Is Here
by Taro Gomi (Chronicle Books)

Spring Is Here: A Barnyard Counting Book
by Pamela Jane (Little Simon)

Wake Up, It's Spring!
by Lisa Campbell Ernst (HarperCollins)

When Will It Be Spring?
by Catherine Walters (Dutton Books)

Three Cheers for April PreK–K, SV 9841-8

Hoppy Spring

Materials

- patterns on page 19
- white and yellow construction paper
- green and light blue craft paper
- pipe cleaners
- markers
- border
- scissors
- pencils
- tape
- stapler

Directions

Teacher Preparation: Duplicate the rabbit patterns on white construction paper. Provide one pattern for each child. Cover the board with the blue craft paper. Cut "grass" out of the green craft paper and staple it to the bottom of the board. Cut out a sun and clouds from construction paper and staple them on the board. Add a festive border and the caption.

1. Cut out a rabbit.

2. Draw a face on the rabbit.

3. Wind a pipe cleaner around a pencil to make a "spring."

4. Slide the pencil out of the pipe cleaner. Stretch the pipe cleaner slightly and tape one end of it to the back of the rabbit.

Staple the free ends of the pipe cleaners to the bulletin board so that the rabbits bounce and jump away from the board.

Spring Centers

Language Center

Language Arts Standard
Recognizes lowercase letters

Flower Fun

Materials

- activity master on page 20
- crayons

Teacher Preparation: Duplicate the activity master to provide one for each student.

Invite children to color the flowers on each row that have the same letters.

Math Center

Math Standard
Counts with understanding and recognizes "how many" in sets of objects

Spotting Butterflies

Materials

- patterns on page 21
- washable markers
- paper towels
- file folders
- spray bottle or wipes
- scissors
- glue

Teacher Preparation: Duplicate, color, and cut out ten butterfly patterns. Draw from one to ten spots on the left wing of each butterfly. Glue the butterflies in a file folder. Make several folders. Laminate the folders.

Have children count the spots on the left wing and draw the same number of dots on the right wing. Challenge them to match the pattern and color on the wings to make both sides look the same. Ask children to wipe the folders clean when they are done.

Spring Centers

Sensory Center

Science Standard
Understands properties
of objects and materials

Muddy Bunnies

Materials

- 2 tubs
- spray bottle
- paper towels
- dirt
- water
- 5 plastic bunnies
- 5 doll shirts

Teacher Preparation: Cover the bottom of one tub with dirt. Add water to the other tub. Fill a spray bottle with water.

Invite children to use the spray bottle to make "rain" by squirting the dirt in the first tub. Ask them to observe how the dirt becomes mud. Then have them use the plastic rabbits to dramatize "Bunnies in the Mud" on page 13. Lead children to understand how both tubs can become mud puddles.

Science Center

Science Standard
Understands the
characteristics of organisms

Spring Is in Bloom

Materials

- containers
- tweezers
- spring flower branches (forsythia, pussy willows, cherry blossoms, redbuds, etc.)
- water
- paper
- hand lens
- crayons

Teacher Preparation: Display three cut branches that show the sequence of growth of the branches: swelling buds, buds, and flowers. Put each branch in a separate container filled with water.

Invite children to observe the different growth phases of the branches. Encourage partners to carefully pull off a bud or flower from each branch. Have children use tweezers to open the buds or flowers and a hand lens to discover what is inside. Then have each child fold a piece of paper in thirds and draw the three different growth phases of the branch. Help children label the different phases.

Spring Centers

Writing Center

Language Arts Standard
Uses context clues while reading and being read to

I See Spring

Materials

- activity masters on pages 22 and 23
- construction paper
- crayons or markers
- stapler
- pencils

Teacher Preparation: Duplicate the activity masters. Make a cover from construction paper and assemble the booklets. Provide a copy for each child.

Lead children in a discussion of changes that happen in the spring. Include such things as weather changes, animals they see, and activities they do. Then invite children to make a booklet that tells about some of the signs of spring. Read aloud the sentences on the booklet pages as children follow along. Have children trace each word and draw and color a picture of the spring symbol. On the last page, have children draw a picture of another spring symbol. Have them dictate or write the word to complete the sentence.

Art Center

Science Standard
Describes orally ways that matter can be put together or changed

Spring Rain Pictures

Materials

- white construction paper
- water
- newspaper
- washable markers
- clothesline
- paper towels
- spray bottle
- clothespins

Teacher Preparation: String a clothesline that is about waist level for children. Then spread a thick layer of newspaper under the clothesline.

Have children draw a springtime picture on the construction paper. Then have them hang the drawing on the clothesline. Invite children to lightly spray the picture with water. Challenge children to describe what happens to the colors as they run and mix.

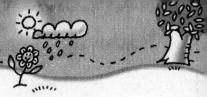

Spring Centers

Puzzle Center

Math Standard
Counts with understanding

Kite Tail Colors

Materials

- pattern on page 24
- scissors
- handmade or storebought color spinner
- construction paper
- beans
- glue

Teacher Preparation: Cover the "tail" section at the top of the page and then duplicate five kite patterns on white construction paper. Trace and cut out five kite tail sections in each of the following colors: red, orange, yellow, green, and blue. Glue the tails on the kites. Color the kites any color, but each kite tail must have a red, an orange, a yellow, a green, and a blue tail section. Make sure the spinner has the same five colors as the kite tails.

Have children take a completed kite and take turns spinning the wheel. They use beans to cover a tail section that matches the color the spinner lands on. If a tail section is already covered, the player misses the turn. The first player to cover all five sections wins. Ask the remaining children to tell how many uncovered sections they had left.

Block Center

Math Standard
Uses familiar manipulatives to recognize shapes and their relationships

Shapes of Spring

Materials

- color shape blocks

Challenge children to use the blocks to form bunnies, flowers, rainbows, umbrellas, and other signs of the season.

Hopping Rabbits Patterns

Use with "Hoppy Spring" on page 14.

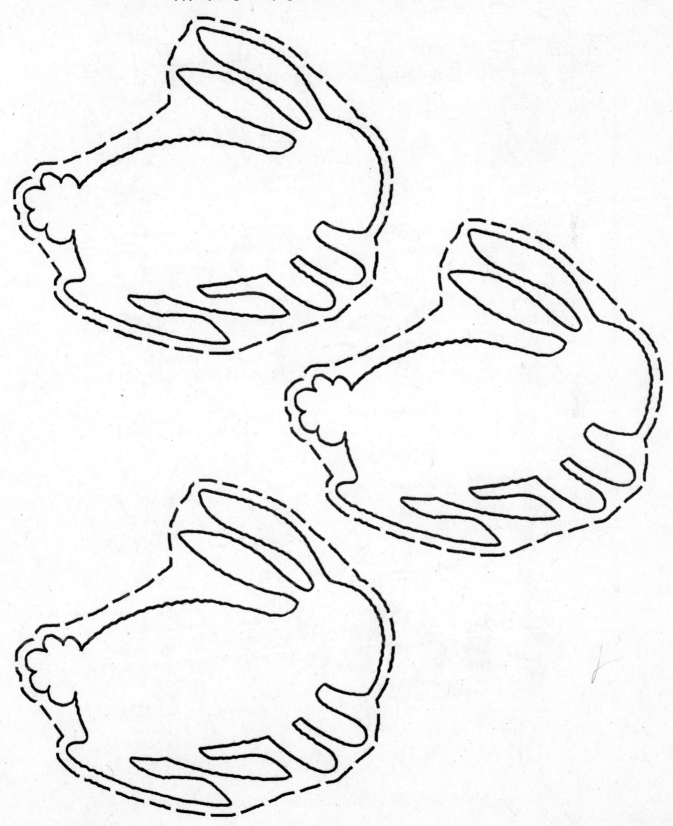

Unit 2, Spring: Patterns
Three Cheers for April PreK–K, SV 9841-8

Name _____

Letter Flowers

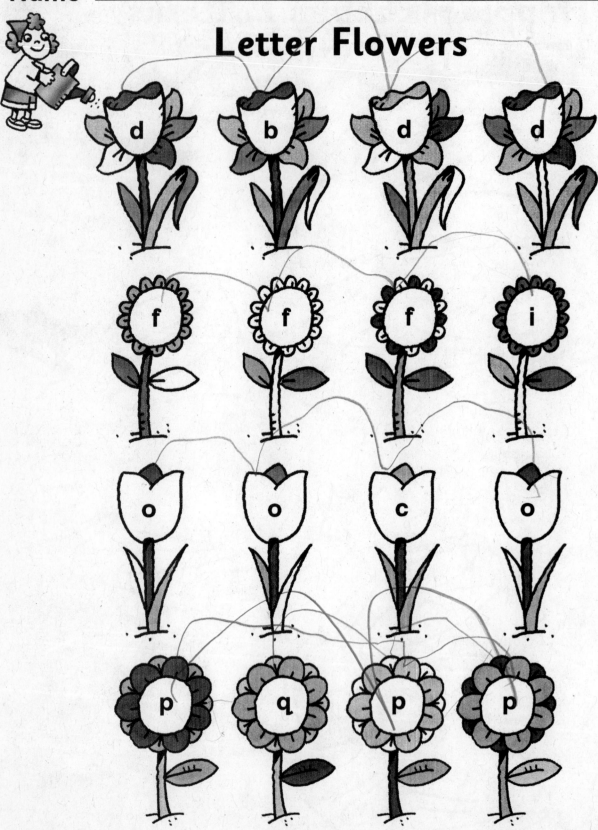

Directions: Use with "Flower Fun" on page 15. Invite children to color the flowers on each row that have the same letters.

Three Cheers for April PreK–K, SV 9841-8

Butterfly Patterns

Use with "Spotting Butterflies" on page 15.

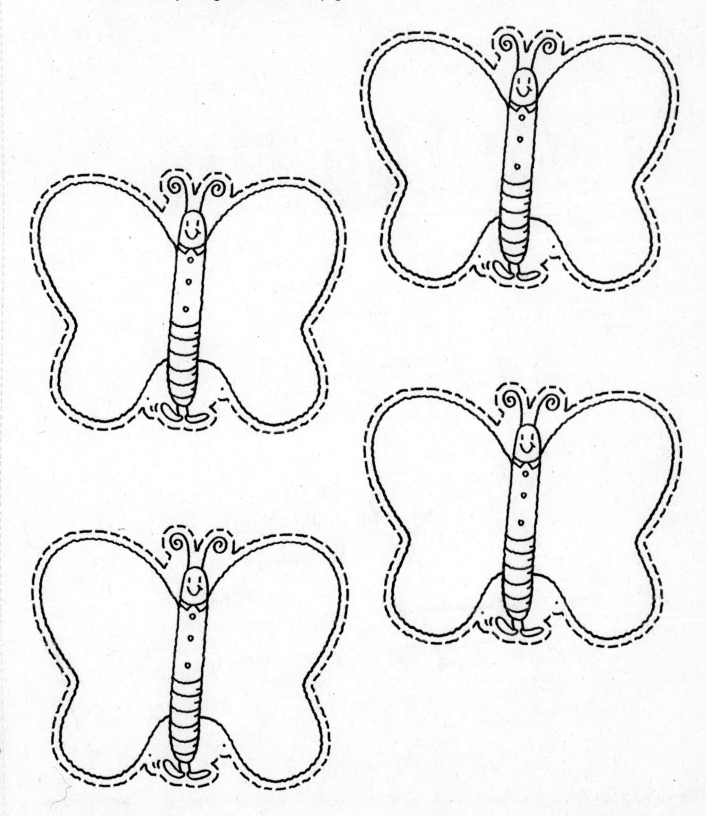

Three Cheers for April PreK–K, SV 9841-8

I See Spring Booklet

Use with "I See Spring" on page 17.

I see a ___bunny___.

1

I see a ___kite___.

2

I See Spring Booklet

Use with "I See Spring" on page 17.

I see _____rain_____.

3

I see _____.

4

Unit 2, Spring: Activity Masters
Three Cheers for April PreK–K, SV 9841-8

Color Kites Game Pattern

Use with "Kite Tail Colors" on page 18.

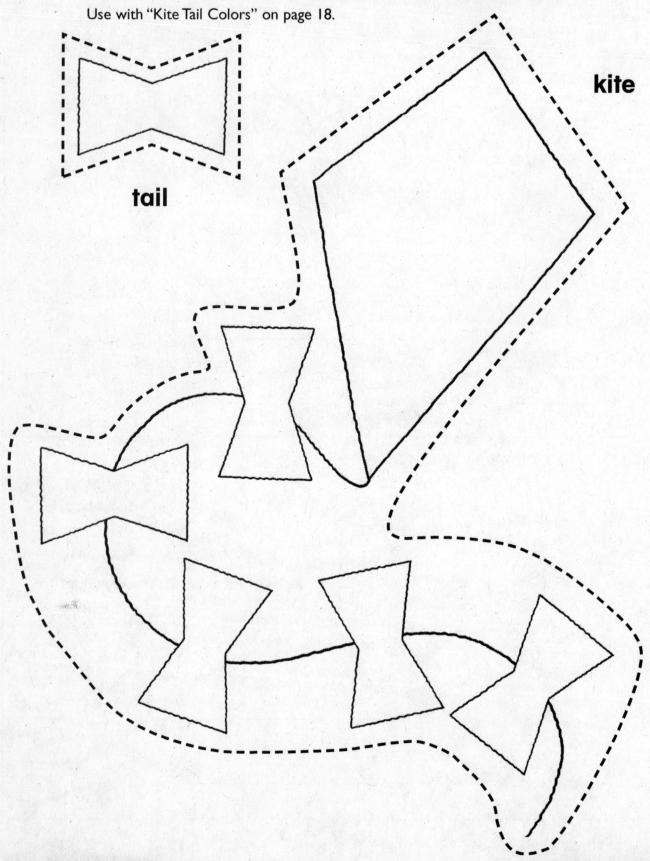

kite

tail

Unit 2, Spring: Patterns
Three Cheers for April PreK–K, SV 9841-8

Seeds of Learning

 Plants have many functions. They change the carbon dioxide humans produce into oxygen. They provide shade, shelter, and food.

 All plants need sun, air, and water to survive.

 The redwood trees on the west coast are the world's tallest trees, reaching heights of 360 feet.

 The largest seed in the world grows on the giant fan palm. It is a single seed and can weigh up to 44 pounds. It takes ten years to grow.

 The slowest growing tree is a white cedar located in Canada. It grew only four inches in height after 155 years.

 The largest flowers grow in Asia. The blooms are three feet across and can weigh up to 24 pounds.

 The tomato is native to the Americas and was first grown by the Aztecs and Incas. Today more tomatoes are eaten in the United States than any other fruit or vegetable.

 The tomato is really a fruit, but a Supreme Court ruling in 1893 legally made it a vegetable.

 Scientists have produced purple carrots and orange cucumbers. These new vegetables have higher concentrations of vitamins, which help change the color.

 It takes nearly six gallons of water to grow a single head of lettuce.

 Thomas Jefferson was the person who first introduced French fries to the United States.

 In South Korea, canned sweet corn is used as an ice cream topping.

Three Cheers for April PreK–K, SV 9841-8

Bean Mosaic Pictures

Materials

- a variety of beans and peas either in separate bags or in bean soup mixes
- small foam plates
- glue
- tweezers (optional)
- wet paper towels

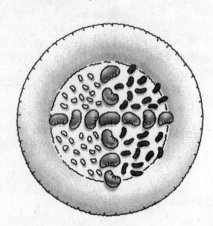

Directions

Teacher Preparation: Sort beans by kind onto separate plates.

1. Spread a thick layer of glue to cover the bottom of a plate.
2. Use the different beans to create simple designs, pictures, and mosaics.

Hairy Harry

Materials

- foam cups
- grass seeds
- soil
- spray bottles
- water
- permanent markers
- spoons
- scissors

Directions

Teacher Preparation: You may wish to have children estimate how many spoonfuls of soil it will take to fill the cup. Remind children to lightly water "Harry" each day.

1. Draw a face on one side of the cup.
2. Spoon dirt into the cup until it is three-quarters full.
3. Sprinkle one teaspoon of grass seed over the soil.
4. Spray water on the grass seed.
5. Place the cups near a window.
6. Lightly water the seeds each day.
7. Give Harry a haircut when the hair grows very long.

Extension: Invite children to play a game. Have them hold empty cups with the toes of their shoes while standing. Have children try to drop four seeds into the cups.

Three Cheers for April PreK–K, SV 9841-8

Garden Soup

You will need

- large soup bone
- 3 qts. water
- 5 beef boullion cubes
- 1 16-oz. can of tomatoes
- 1 stalk of chopped celery
- 1 chopped onion
- 1 T. pepper
- 1 16-oz. can mixed vegetables
- 1 16-oz. can green beans
- 1 16-oz. can peas
- 1 16-oz. can corn
- 1 bag of frozen plain French fries
- 3 T. salt
- 1 T. chili powder
- crock pot
- large spoon
- can openers that leave edges dull
- bowls
- spoons
- plastic knife

Directions

Teacher Preparation: Let the fries thaw slightly. Invite children to take turns opening cans and stirring the soup when supervised.

1. Put the first seven ingredients in a crock pot and cook on high for an hour.

2. Open the remaining cans and pour them into the crock pot.

3. Cut the fries into bite-size pieces and add them to the broth.

4. Stir in the salt and chili powder.

5. Heat the crock pot on high for two hours.

6. Serve the soup in bowls and discuss the kinds of vegetables in the soup.

Note: Be aware of children who may have food allergies.

This Is the Way We Plant the Seeds

(Tune: "Here We Go 'Round the Mulberry Bush")

This is the way we dig the hole,   (pantomime digging with a hand shovel)
Dig the hole, dig the hole.
This is the way we dig the hole
In a springtime garden!

This is the way we plant the seeds . . .   (pantomime planting seeds)

This is the way we water the seeds . . .   (pantomime watering seeds
                                             with a watering can)

This is the way the seeds will grow . . .   (hold hand out, palm-side down,
                                             near ground and lift)

This is the way we pick the peas . . .   (pantomime picking peas)

This is the way we shell the peas . . .   (pantomime shelling peas)

This is the way we cook the peas . . .   (pantomime shaking a pan)

This is the way we eat the peas . . .   (pantomime eating)

Dig into These Books

From Seed to Plant
by Gail Gibbons (Holiday House)

Gardens
by Gail Gibbons (Holiday House)

Growing Vegetable Soup
by Lois Ehlert (Voyager Books)

How a Seed Grows
by Helene J. Jordan (HarperTrophy)

In the Garden of Abdul Gasazi
by Chris Van Allsburg (Houghton
Mifflin Company)

Jack's Garden
by Henry Cole (HarperTrophy)

Planting a Rainbow
by Lois Ehlert (Voyager Books)

The Tiny Seed
by Eric Carle (Aladdin Library)

A Tree Is a Plant
by Clyde Robert Bulla (HarperTrophy)

Three Cheers for April PreK–K, SV 9841-8

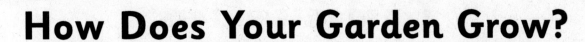

How Does Your Garden Grow?

Materials

- patterns on pages 34 and 35
- children's pictures
- light blue craft paper
- construction paper
- large craft sticks
- green markers
- glue
- stapler
- scissors

Directions

Teacher Preparation: Enlarge and cut out a sun, cloud, and wind pattern for the bulletin board. Duplicate and cut out multiple yellow suns, gray clouds, and white winds the same size as the patterns to create a patterned border around the bulletin board. Using the flower pattern pieces, trace and cut out a yellow center, five petals of various colors, and two green leaves for each child. (Children can choose to make the flower one color or multi-colored.) Cover the bulletin board in light blue paper. Staple the sun, cloud, and wind on the board. Add the caption.

1. Color the craft stick green.

2. Glue a yellow center on one end of the stick.

3. Glue five petals around the center.

4. Glue the picture of child's face in the flower center.

5. Glue two leaves to the bottom of the stick.

Have children identify the pattern in the border. Explain that all plants need sun, air, and water to live. Then help children staple their flowers to the board.

Three Cheers for April PreK–K, SV 9841-8

Garden Centers

Math Center

Math Standard
Knows that ordinal numbers show position

Orderly Garden

Materials

- activity master on page 36
- crayons
- scissors

Teacher Preparation: Duplicate the page for each child. Or for younger children, duplicate the page once, cut the pictures apart to make individual cards, and color the pictures.

Have children write 1, 2, or 3 to show the sequence of each group of pictures. Or have children put individual picture cards in sequential order.

Language Center

Language Arts Center
Identifies beginning sounds

Rhyme Around the Roses

Materials

- picture cards on pages 37 and 38
- crayons or markers
- construction paper
- scissors

Teacher Preparation: Duplicate the 18 picture cards on construction paper. Color and cut apart the pictures.

Review the names of the pictures shown on the cards. Have children identify the pictures that are associated with the garden. Then invite children to match pictures whose names rhyme or begin with the same sound. The following pictures cards match beginning letter sounds: corn/cane, horn/hose, rose/rain/run, sun/seeds, boy/beads/bees, peas/pig, child/chair/chief.

Garden Centers

Dramatic Play Center

Math Standard
Sorts or classifies by color

Flower Shop

Materials

- plastic pots
- plastic flowers
- clay or play dough

Encourage children to divide the flowers into groups according to color. Invite children to arrange the flowers in pots to make beautiful springtime arrangements.

Block Center

Math Standard
Sorts or classifies by kind

Garden Plantings

Materials

- tape
- pictures of individual fruits, vegetables, and flowers

Teacher Preparation: Tape a picture of each fruit, vegetable, or flower on a block.

Have children plan a garden by laying the blocks on the floor. Encourage them to organize the garden so all fruits, vegetables, and flowers are together.

Garden Centers

Writing Center

Language Arts Standard
Begins to form letters correctly with manipulatives

I "Seed" My Name

Materials

- a variety of seeds
- permanent marker
- tag board
- glue

Teacher Preparation: Write each child's name in large letters on a piece of tag board.

Ask children to trace the first letter of their name with glue. Have them press seeds in the glue to "write" the letter. Have them repeat the process with each letter. Ask them to set the names aside to dry.

Science Center

Science Standard
Understands characteristics of organisms

Helping Plants Grow

Materials

- activity master on page 39
- glue
- crayons
- scissors

Teacher Preparation: Duplicate the activity master.

Invite children to color the picture. Help them read the words at the bottom of the page. Then ask them to cut apart the words. Have them match and glue the words to each picture to show what plants need to grow.

Garden Centers

Sensory Center

Seed Sort

Materials

- tub
- tweezers
- sunflower seeds
- foam plates
- a variety of beans, peas, and seeds (either in separate bags or in bean soup mixes)

Teacher Preparation: Fill the tub with the beans, peas, and seeds.

Have children sort the beans, peas, and seeds onto separate plates. Use the beans for the "Bean Mosaic Pictures" on page 26.

Reading Center

Seed and Read

Materials

- pocket chart
- self-stick magnetic tape
- scissors
- metal cake pans
- packages of fruit, vegetable, and flower seeds

Teacher Preparation: Cut pieces of the magnetic tape and stick a piece to the back of each seed package. Place each seed package in a pocket of the chart.

Invite children to go "shopping" for seeds. Have them choose the packages they would like to purchase for a garden and place them in their metal "baskets."

Plants Need . . . Patterns

Use with "How Does Your Garden Grow?" on page 29.

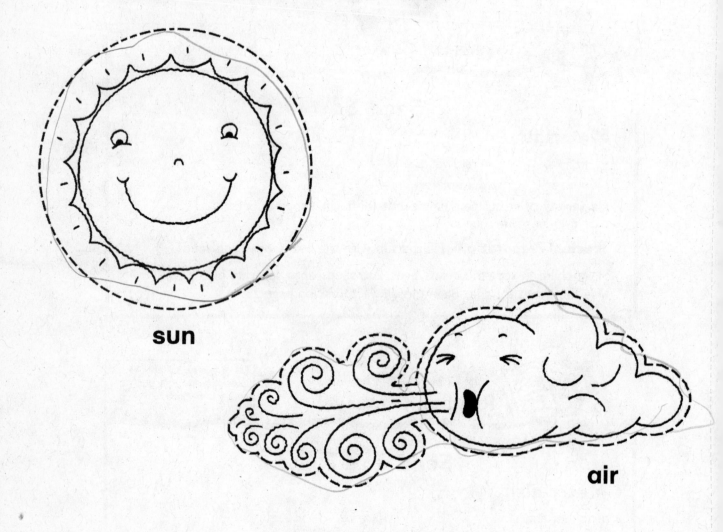

sun

air

water

Three Cheers for April PreK–K, SV 9841-8

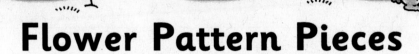

Flower Pattern Pieces
Use with "How Does Your Garden Grow?" on page 29.

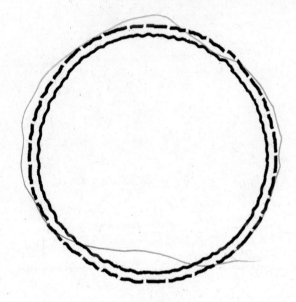

center

petal

leaf

Three Cheers for April PreK–K, SV 9841-8

Name _____

From Seed to Me

_____

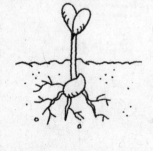

_____

_____

Directions: Use with "Orderly Garden" on page 30. Have children write *1*, *2*, or *3* to show the sequence of each group of pictures. Or have children put individual picture cards in sequential order.

Unit 3, Gardens: Activity Master
Three Cheers for April PreK–K, SV 9841-8

Rhyming Cards

Use with "Rhyme Around the Roses" on page 30.

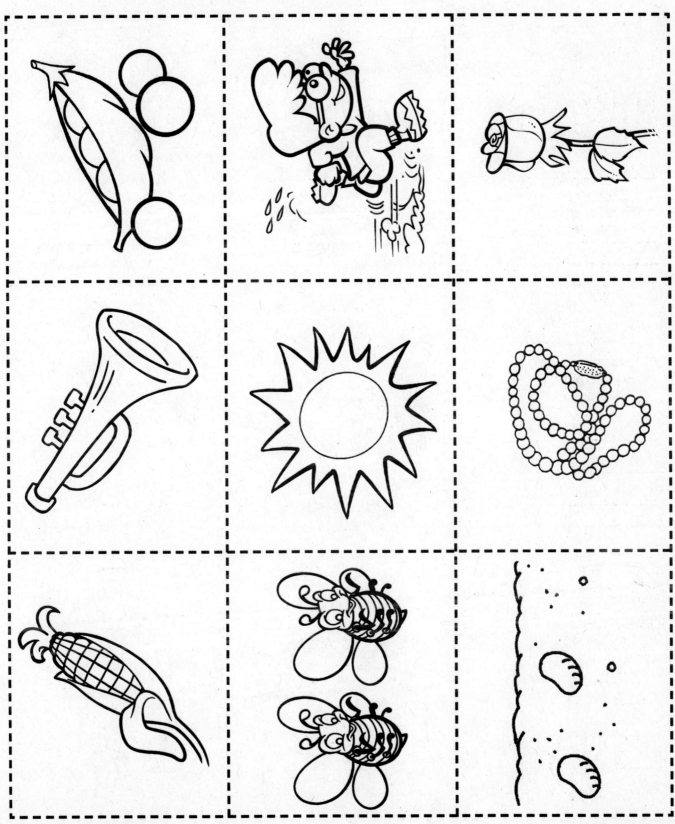

Rhyming Cards

Use with "Rhyme Around the Roses" on page 30.

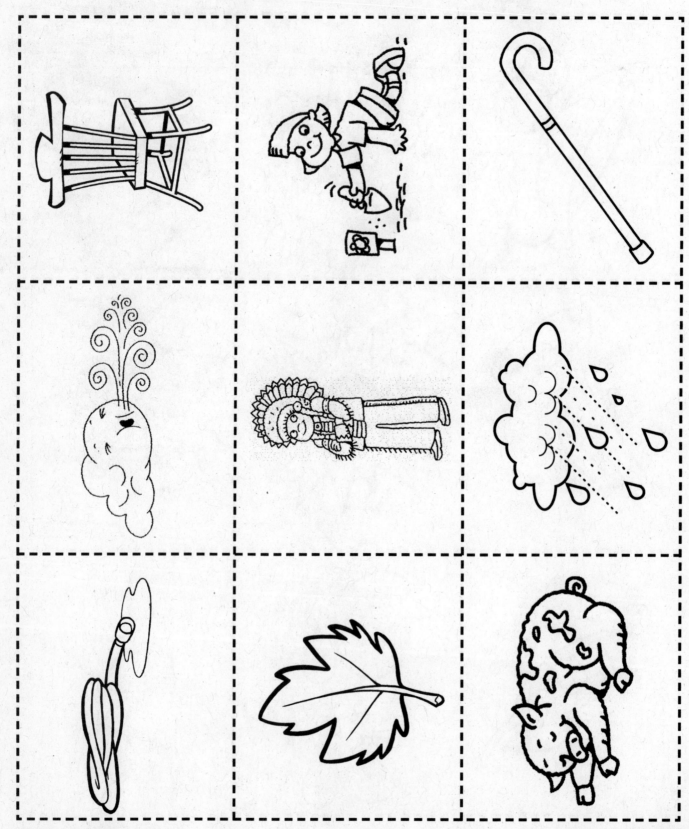

Three Cheers for April PreK–K, SV 9841-8

Name _____

Plant Helpers

| sun | water | air |

Directions: Use with "Helping Plants Grow" on page 32. Invite children to color the picture. Help them read the words at the bottom of the page. Then ask them to cut apart the words. Have them match and glue the words under the picture that shows what plants need to grow.

Eggs-tra Good Information

A female alligator makes a nest by using sticks, leaves, and mud to form a mound. Then she digs down one to two feet to lay the eggs. The alligator then covers the nest and lies on it. Before babies hatch, they begin to chirp. At that time, the female alligator will dig up the eggs.

Alligators stay with their young once hatched. A female alligator will carry her babies in her mouth.

Some turtles can lay up to 230 eggs in one nest.

Evidence shows that the temperature of some incubating turtle eggs determines if the babies will be mostly male or female. Higher temperatures produce more females, while lower temperatures produce more males.

Some snakes lay eggs in nests. Other snakes keep and hatch the eggs inside their bodies. The babies are born alive.

A reptile eggshell is very tough. It keeps heat and moisture in and predators out. Many reptile babies have an egg tooth on the end of their snout that helps them cut through the hard eggshell.

The hummingbird lays the smallest egg. It is about the size of a jellybean.

The ostrich lays the largest egg. It is about the size of a large grapefruit.

The color of an egg depends on where it is laid. Eggs look like the nest to keep them safe from predators.

Fish and amphibians lay their eggs in large masses in water. The eggs are wrapped in a jelly-like substance to protect them from diseases. However, water can pass through each egg to give oxygen to the embryo.

Three Cheers for April PreK–K, SV 9841-8

All Cracked Up

Materials

- egg pattern on page 49
- white construction paper
- brads
- crayons
- scissors
- glue

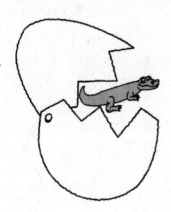

Directions

Teacher Preparation: Duplicate and cut out two egg patterns from construction paper for each child.

1. Draw and color a picture of an animal that hatches on one egg.

2. Cut apart the other egg, using zigzag cuts to make the egg look cracked.

3. Glue the bottom part of the cracked egg on the first egg, matching the edges.

4. Overlap the top part of the cracked egg over the bottom. Push a brad through one side of the eggs, going through all the thicknesses, and spread the prongs on the back side.

Nesting Birds

Materials

- patterns on page 50
- small brown paper bags
- white construction paper
- dry tempera paint
- cotton balls
- crayons or markers
- newspapers
- glue
- scissors
- plastic bags

Directions

Teacher Preparation: Duplicate the patterns. Identify a bird that the children might see that week and do research to find the egg color of that bird. Pour the same color of dry paint in a plastic bag and add the cotton balls. Shake the bag to color the cotton balls. Remove them and shake excess paint off. Take children on a walk and point out different kinds of birds, particularly the bird that you researched. Discuss the items that birds use to make a nest. Ask children to pretend to be birds and collect items from the ground that they would use in a nest. Have children put the items in plastic bags.

1. Empty the plastic bag on newspaper.

2. Roll the top of the paper bag down, leaving about two inches on the bottom.

3. Glue the items gathered on the walk to the inside of the bag to make a bird's nest.

4. Glue two cotton ball "eggs" inside the nest.

5. Color and cut out a bird.

6. Perch the bird in the nest.

"Quacked" Eggs

You will need

- frozen rolls
- small plastic birds that are safe for baking (or other animals that hatch)
- plastic wrap
- spray shortening
- baking trays
- paper plates
- oven

Directions

1. Defrost the rolls according to the package directions.

2. Flatten a roll and place a plastic bird in the center.

3. Fold the dough over the bird and roll the dough into a ball.

4. Place the roll on a baking tray, cover with plastic wrap that has been sprayed with shortening, and set aside in a warm place to rise for two hours.

5. Bake the rolls according to the directions.

Note: Be aware of children who may have food allergies. Have children remove the plastic birds from the baked rolls before eating the rolls.

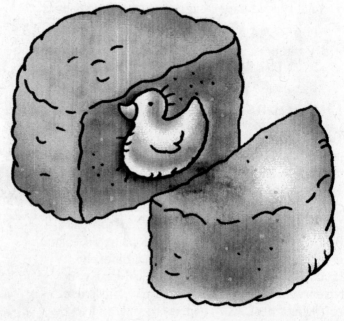

Unit 4, Eggs-actly Eggs: Kid's Kitchen
Three Cheers for April PreK–K, SV 9841-8

♫ I'm a Little Baby Chick

(Tune: "I'm a Little Tea Pot")

I'm a little baby chick   (crouch in a ball)

Growing in an egg.

Here is my head   (shake head)

And here is my leg.   (shake leg)

When I've filled the shell,   (stretch out arms)

It's hatching time.

Tap! Tap! CRACK!   (tap floor twice, then clap)

And out I climb!   (stand and take a step forward)

I'm a baby alligator . . .

I'm a baby turtle . . .

I'm a baby turkey . . .

I'm a baby caterpillar . . .

I'm a baby grasshopper . . .

Crack Open These Books!

Chickens Aren't the Only Ones
by Ruth Heller (Grosset and Dunlap)

The Chicken's Child
by Margaret A. Hartellus (Scholastic)

From Tadpole to Frog
by Wendy Pfefer (HarperTrophy)

An Extraordinary Egg
by Leo Lionni (Alfred A. Knopf)

The Golden Egg Book
by Margaret Wise Brown (Western Publishing)

Horton Hatches the Egg
by Dr. Seuss (Random House)

A Nest Full of Eggs
by Priscilla Belz Jenkins (HarperTrophy)

Tracks in the Sand
by Loreen Leedy (Doubleday)

Who's Hatching?

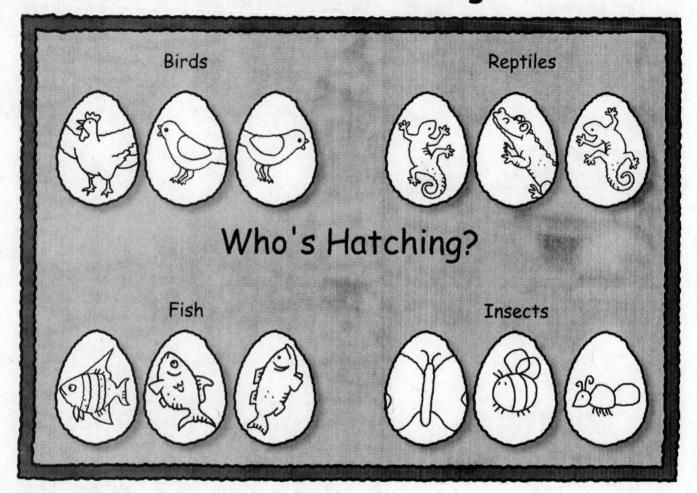

Birds

Reptiles

Who's Hatching?

Fish

Insects

Materials

- animal cards on pages 52 and 53
- patterns on page 54
- white construction paper
- crayons
- craft paper
- border
- glue
- scissors
- stapler

Directions

Teacher Preparation: Duplicate the egg patterns on construction paper and provide one for each child. Duplicate several copies of the animal cards and cut them apart. Cover the board with the craft paper. Add a festive border, the category names, and the caption.

1. Choose a card of an animal that hatches.

2. Color the animal.

3. Glue the animal on an egg.

Have children identify their animal and tell which group the animal belongs to—birds, reptiles, fish, or insects. Staple the animal with the correct group on the board.

Eggs-treme Centers

Language Center

Language Arts Standard
Knows the alphabetical order of letters

Alphabet Eggs

Materials

- activity master on page 51
- crayons

Teacher Preparation: Duplicate the activity master.

Remind children that a frog can lay lots of eggs at one time and that frogs hatch as tadpoles. Have children create a path by coloring the eggs in alphabetical order.

Math Center

Math Standard
Makes reasonable estimates

Estimating Eggs

Materials

- plastic eggs
- baskets in various sizes

Have children work in pairs to estimate the number of eggs that will fit in each basket. Then have them check their guesses.

Eggs-treme Centers

Sensory Center

Science Standard
Understands organisms
and their environment

Eggs in the Sand

Materials

- tub
- sand
- table-tennis balls

Teacher Preparation: Fill the tub with sand.

Point out that turtle eggs look like table-tennis balls. Then explain that sea turtles climb on the beach at night, dig a hole, lay their eggs, and then bury their eggs before returning to the sea. Invite children to take turns burying the "turtle eggs" for others to find. Be sure to caution children that if they see real turtle eggs, they are to leave them alone.

Science Center

Science Standard
Understands characteristics
of organisms

Bird, Reptile, Fish, or Insect?

Materials

- animal cards on pages 52 and 53
- white construction paper
- markers
- scissors

Teacher Preparation: Duplicate on construction paper, color, and cut out the animal cards.

Remind children that most birds, reptiles, fish, and insects begin life in eggs. Then discuss the characteristics that define each group. Have children sort the animal cards into the appropriate groups.

Eggs-treme Centers

Music Center

Science Standard
Understands position and motion of objects

Shaker Sort

Materials

- 12 plastic eggs of the same color
- 2 marbles
- large paper clips
- water
- egg carton
- 2 small bells
- 2 pennies
- sand
- permanent glue

Teacher Preparation: Fill two eggs with the same materials. For example, put one marble in each of two eggs, a bell in another pair of eggs, sand in a third pair of eggs, etc. Then seal the eggs with permanent glue. Put the eggs in the egg carton.

Invite children to shake each egg and find the partner egg filled with the same material.

Art Center

Language Arts Standard
Uses simple sentences to communicate thoughts and ideas when speaking

Egg-stra Shiny Eggs

Materials

- pattern on page 49
- food coloring
- 12" x 18" white construction paper
- can opener (the kind that removes the sharp edges)
- condensed milk
- paintbrushes

Teacher Preparation: Enlarge pattern to fit on the white construction paper. Then duplicate the egg on construction paper to provide one for each child. Open the milk cans and mix one color of food coloring in each. Stir to mix, adding more coloring if desired.

Have children paint the eggs using the mixture. Invite children to describe the texture (shiny) when the eggs are dry.

Eggs-treme Centers

Game Center

Math Standard
Counts with understanding

Little Chick Pick Up

Materials

- yellow cotton balls
- kitchen tongs
- orange paper
- wiggly eyes
- glue
- scissors
- large nest (made from a brown bag or the bottom of a milk jug)

Teacher Preparation: Cut small triangles from the orange paper. Glue one on each cotton ball to make a chick. Next glue two wiggly eyes on each chick. Put the chicks in the nest.

Ask children to gently toss the chicks out of the nest. Have them use the tongs to collect the escaping chicks. Have children count the chicks as they collect them.

Puzzle Center

Math Standard
Applies and adapts a variety of appropriate strategies to solve problems

Cracked Eggs

Materials

- patterns on page 54
- poster board
- scissors

Teacher Preparation: Enlarge each egg puzzle pattern and trace it on poster board. Cut the eggs into puzzle pieces.

Have children put each puzzle together.

Egg Pattern

Use with "All Cracked Up" on page 41 and "Egg-stra Shiny Eggs" on page 47.

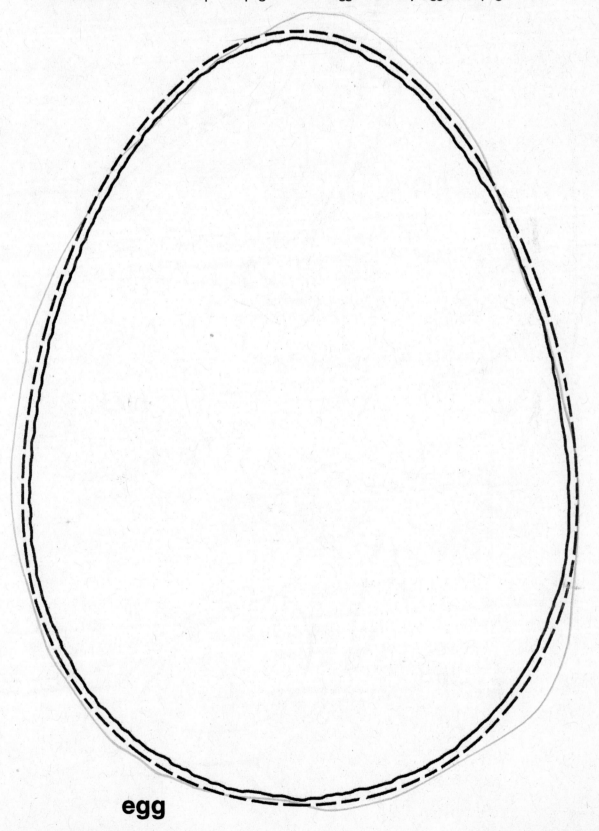

egg

Unit 4, Eggs-actly Eggs: Pattern
Three Cheers for April PreK–K, SV 9841-8

Bird Patterns

Use with "Nesting Birds" on page 41.

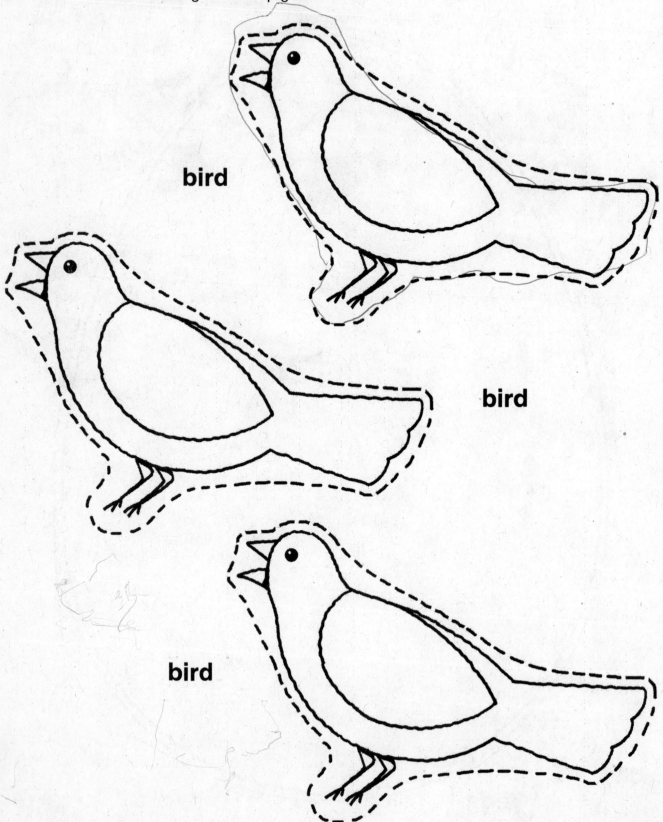

bird

bird

bird

y

Eggs-tra Eggs

Directions: Use with "Alphabet Eggs" on page 45. Have children create a path by coloring the eggs in alphabetical order.

Three Cheers for April PreK–K, SV 9841-8

Animal Cards

Use with "Who's Hatching?" on page 44 and "Bird, Reptile, Fish, or Insect?" on page 46.

turkey

grasshopper

robin

ant

duck

mosquito

chicken

butterfly

Three Cheers for April PreK–K, SV 9841-8

Animal Cards

Use with "Who's Hatching?" on page 44 and "Bird, Reptile, Fish, or Insect?" on page 46.

alligator	sailfish
gecko	perch
turtle	goldfish
snake	angel fish

Egg Puzzles Patterns
Use with "Who's Hatching?" on page 44 and "Cracked Eggs" on page 48.

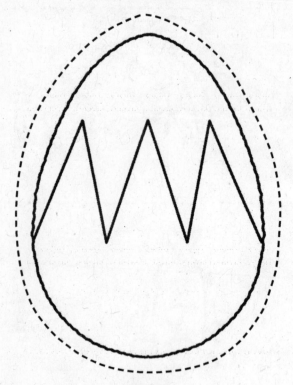

egg

egg

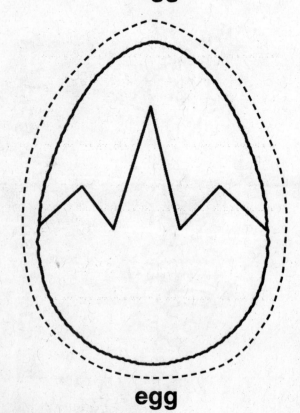

egg

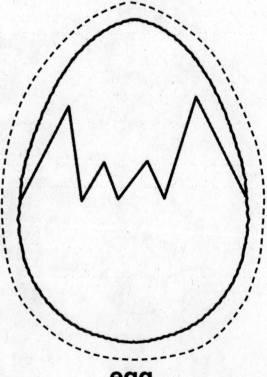

egg

Unit 4, Eggs-actly Eggs: Patterns
Three Cheers for April PreK–K, SV 9841-8

Talking Trash . . .

 Earth Day is an American celebration in which people work to clean up the natural resources, as well as to raise the awareness of the needs of the environment.

 It is important to teach children the three *R's*: reduce (use less of), reuse (find a way to use an item without changing it), and recycle (change an item so it can be used again).

 Senator Gaylord Nelson proposed the idea in 1969, and Earth Day was first publicly celebrated on April 22, 1970.

 It takes 50 to 80 years for a plastic cup to disintegrate.

 There are several kinds of pollution: noise, air, water, and land.

 Over 500,000 trees are used to make all the Sunday newspapers.

 People in the United States throw away so much aluminum that the amount tossed in three months could build all the commercial airplanes.

 Scientists have found a way to make a fleece-like fabric from plastic bottles.

 Americans recycle nearly 50% of the aluminum used.

 The average American throws away six pounds of tin and two pounds of plastic every month.

 About 41% of trash thrown away by Americans is made out of paper.

Unit 5, Our Earth: Teacher Information
Three Cheers for April PreK–K, SV 9841-8

Earth Pictures

Materials

- coffee filters
- markers
- spray bottle
- water
- black construction paper
- foil star stickers
- glue
- newspaper

Directions

Teacher Preparation: Fill the spray bottle with water.

1. Scribble blue lines all over the filter to represent Earth's oceans. Some white should still be showing.

2. Make two or three green dots in different places on the filter to represent land on Earth.

3. Place the filter on newspaper.

4. Lightly spray water on the filter to make the colors bleed together.

5. When the filter is dry, glue it on black paper.

6. Put the star stickers around "Earth."

Jug Scoop and Paper Ball

Materials

- clean, plastic milk jugs
- variety of stickers
- newspaper
- masking tape
- scissors

Directions

Teacher Preparation: For each child, cut a jug to remove the area from below the handle to part of the bottom. Remind children about the importance of reusing items to help Earth.

1. Put stickers on the outside of the milk jug for decoration.

2. Crush a sheet of newspaper into a ball.

3. Wrap tape around the newspaper to help the ball keep its shape.

Use these items to play "Super Scooper" on page 62.

Land and Water Earth

You will need

- blue gelatin mix
- water
- chocolate sandwich cookies
- chocolate pudding mix
- milk
- clear, plastic cups
- muffin tins
- clay
- measuring cups
- spoons
- bowls

Directions

Teacher Preparation: Prepare pudding and gelatin according to the package. You may wish to have children help prepare these foods.

1. Pour one-half cup of blue gelatin into a clear cup for the ocean.

2. Roll some clay into a one-inch ball and place in a muffin cup.

3. Press the cup into the clay at an angle so that the gelatin will be slanted when set, but the cup will not move.

4. Refrigerate the gelatin until set.

5. Crush a cookie in a bowl for rocks.

6. Add two large spoonfuls of pudding for soil and stir the rocks and soil together.

7. Gently spoon the rocks and dirt over the gelatin ocean.

Note: Be aware of children who may have food allergies.

Earth Cheer

Pick up the trash.

Then plant a tree.

Keep the Earth clean

For you and me!

Sort the bottles,

Plastics, and cans.

It's time for us

To give Earth a hand!

Extension Activity

Trace the megaphone pattern on page 64 on tag board for each child. Let children color the megaphone, cut it out, and tape the sides together to form a cone. Then invite children to chant the Earth Cheer using their megaphones.

Pick Up These Books

The Earth and I
by Frank Asch (Harcourt)

Earth Day Birthday
by Pattie L. Schnetzler (Dawn Publications)

Earth Day–Hooray!
by Stuart J. Murphy (HarperTrophy)

**The Great Kapok Tree:
A Tale of the Amazon Forest**
by Lynne Cherry (Voyager Books)

The Great Trash Bash
by Loreen Leedy (Holiday House)

Recycles
by Gail Gibbons (Little, Brown & Company)

The Wartville Wizard
by Don Madden (Aladdin Library)

Where Does the Garbage Go?
by Paul Showers (HarperTrophy)

Give Earth a Hand!

Materials

- patterns on pages 65 and 66
- yellow craft paper
- white construction paper
- overhead projector
- transparency
- blue and green tempera paints
- border
- sponge brushes
- paint containers
- crayons
- scissors
- stapler

Directions

Teacher Preparation: Make a transparency of the Earth pattern. Duplicate and cut out the hand patterns from white construction paper. Cover the board with the craft paper. Use the overhead projector and the transparency to trace a large Earth in the center of the bulletin board. Paint the Earth. Add a festive border and the caption.

1. Draw a picture on the hand cutout of one way to help Earth.

2. Write or dictate a sentence to go along with the picture.

Invite children to share their ideas during circle time. Then help children staple their hand art to the bulletin board.

Recycling Centers

Math Center

Math Standard
Associates numerals up to 10 with sets of objects

Endangered Animal Count

Materials

- activity master on page 67
- crayons

Teacher Preparation: Duplicate the activity master.

Lead children in a discussion of animals that are on the endangered list. Then have children color and count the animals. Ask them to circle the number to show how many animals are in each group.

Language Center

Language Arts Standards
Recognizes uppercase and lowercase letters

Letter Perfect Recycling

Materials

- patterns on page 68
- scissors
- file folder
- glue
- markers

Teacher Preparation: Duplicate, color, and cut out the patterns. Glue the bins on the inside of a file folder. Write a capital letter on each bin. Write the corresponding lowercase letters on the recyclable items.

Have children match the lowercase letters to the capital letters to find in which bin each recycled item belongs.

Extension: For a phonemic awareness activity, draw or cut out pairs of pictures whose names have the same ending sounds. For example, cut out magazine pictures of a fox and the number six. Glue one picture on a bin and the other on a recyclable item. Children match the item to a bin by listening for the ending /ks/ sound.

Recycling Centers

Dramatic Play Center

Math Standard
Sorts or classifies by kind

Sorting to Recycle

Materials

- patterns on page 68
- white construction paper
- 4 boxes
- tape
- scissors
- markers or crayons
- recyclable items: clean plastic bottles, cans, boxes, magazines, newspaper, cardboard tubes, etc.

Teacher Preparation: Duplicate, color, and cut out the recyclable item patterns. Tape the pictures to three boxes to show which hold paper, plastic, and cans. Put all the recyclable items in the fourth box.

Invite children to sort the recyclable items into the appropriate boxes.

Reading Center

Language Arts Standard
Begins to use word recognition strategies, with support

Continents and Ocean

Materials

- world map
- globe
- tape

Teacher Preparation: Tape the map on the wall.

Challenge children to match continent and ocean names found on the map to those on the globe.

Recycling Centers

Art Center

Math Standard
Uses familiar manipulatives to recognize shapes and their relationships

From Trash to Treasure

Materials

- scrap construction paper
- glue
- scissors
- tape
- interesting art supplies, such as yarn, ribbon, and buttons
- clean plastic bottles, cans, boxes, egg cartons, and cardboard tubes in a variety of sizes

Invite children to use their imaginations to make animals, toys, games, and other interesting items using the materials in the center.

Game Center

Math Standard
Counts with understanding

Super Scooper

Materials

- scoops and balls (completed in "Jug Scoop and Paper Ball" on page 56)

Challenge children to work with a partner to count how many times in a row they can toss the ball to each other and catch it in the scoops.

Recycling Centers

Block Center

Math Standard
Uses familiar manipulatives to recognize shapes and their relationships

Reused Blocks

Materials

- clean cans, boxes, and cardboard tubes in a variety of sizes

Have children build with the recycled materials.

Science Center

Science Standard
Understands changes in environments

Pollution Detectives

Materials

- activity master on page 69
- crayons

Teacher Preparation: Duplicate the activity master.

Remind children that there are several kinds of pollution: noise, air, land, and water. Then have them color the parts of the picture that show pollution.

Megaphone Pattern

Use with "Earth Cheer" on page 58.

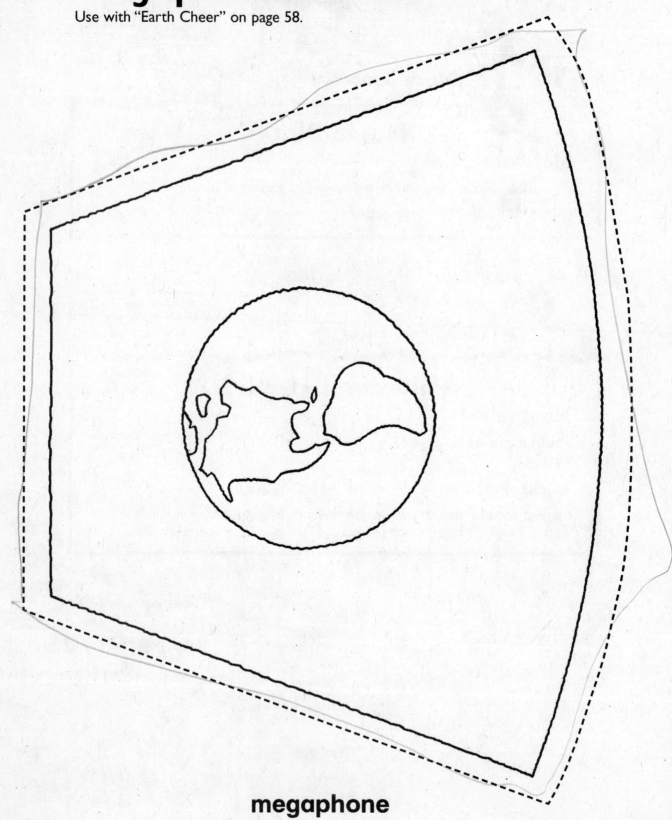

megaphone

Earth Pattern

Use with "Give Earth a Hand!" on page 59.

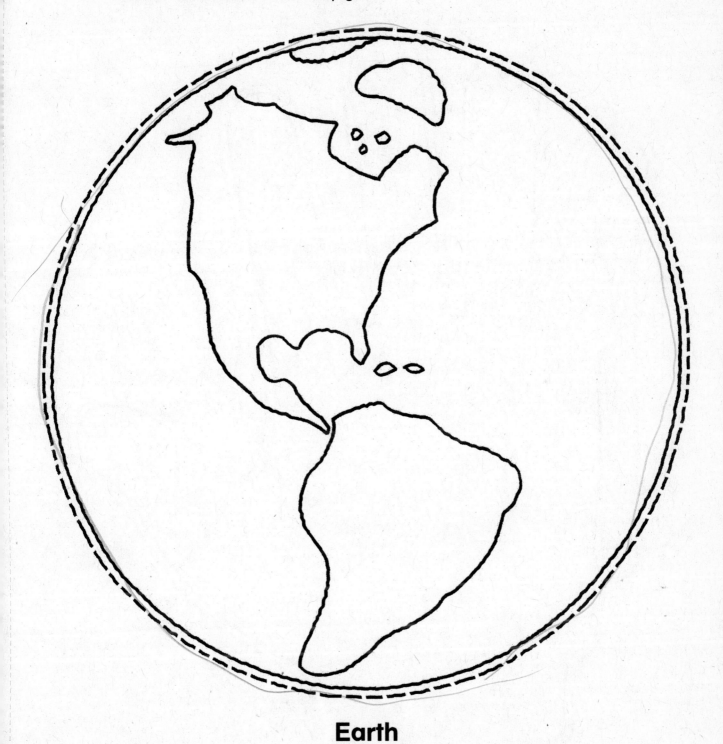

Earth

Hand Pattern

Use with "Give Earth a Hand!" on page 59.

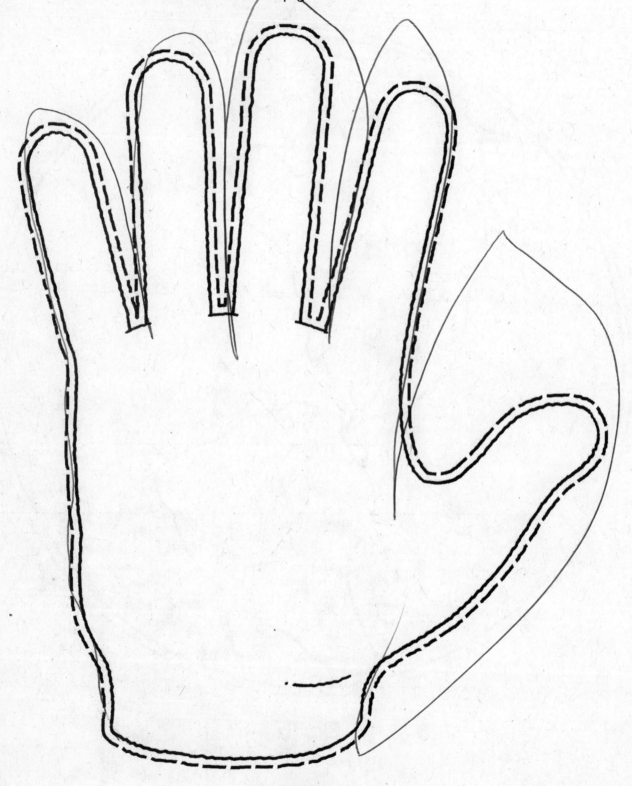

hand

Unit 5, Our Earth: Pattern
Three Cheers for April PreK–K, SV 9841-8

Name _____

Animal Count

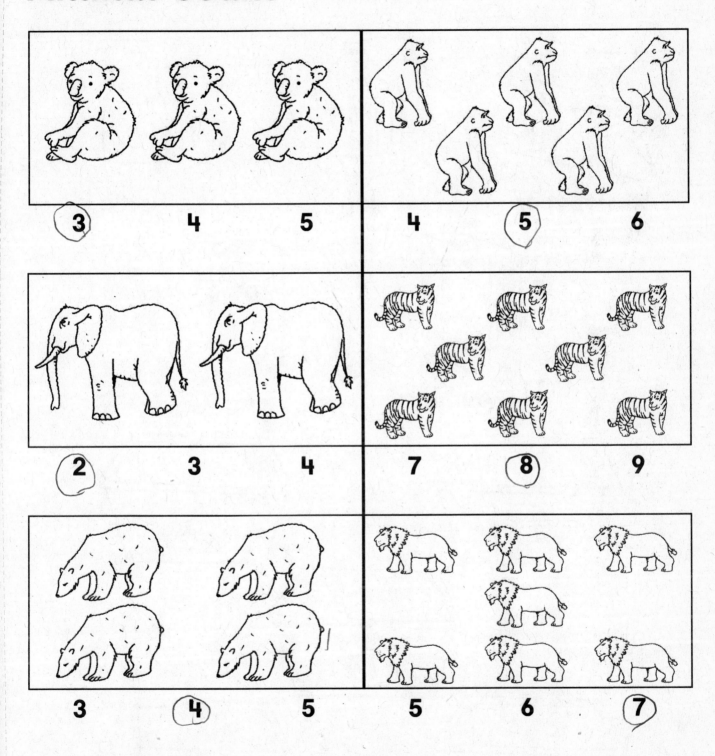

Directions: Use with "Endangered Animal Count" on page 60. Have children color and count the animals. Ask them to circle the number to show how many animals are in each group.

Unit 5, Our Earth: Activity Master
Three Cheers for April PreK–K, SV 9841-8

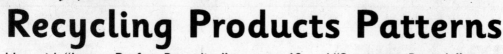

Recycling Products Patterns

Use with "Letter Perfect Recycling" on page 60 and "Sorting to Recycle" on page 61.

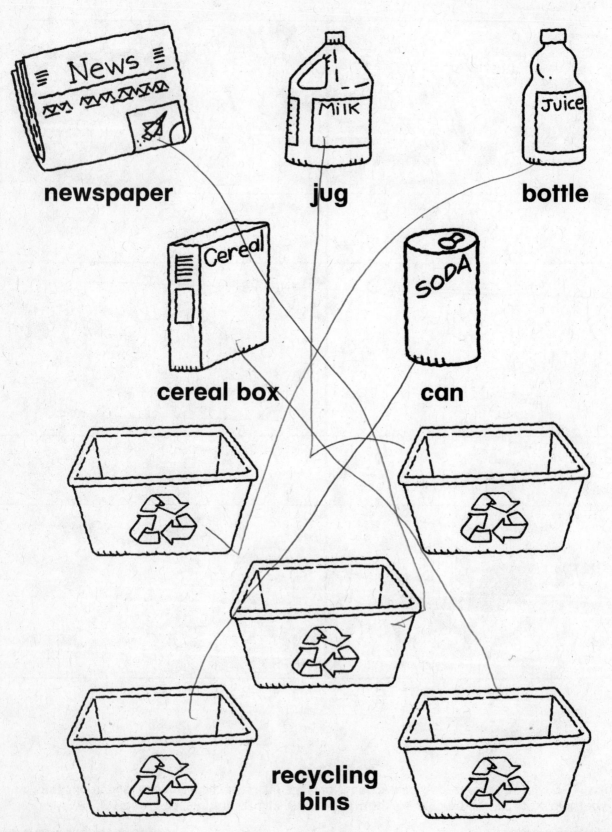

newspaper

jug

bottle

cereal box

can

recycling
bins

Unit 5, Our Earth: Patterns
Three Cheers for April PreK–K, SV 9841-8

Pollution Hunt

Directions: Use with "Pollution Detectives" on page 63. Remind children that there are several kinds of pollution: noise, air, land, and water. Then have them color the parts of the picture that show pollution.

Three Cheers for April PreK–K, SV 9841-8

Moo-velous News from the Farm

 Pigs are not able to sweat; that's why they lie in water and mud to stay cool. Some farmers use sprinklers to keep their pigs cool.

 Goats don't have front teeth on the upper part of their mouths.

 A sheep can produce enough wool in one shearing to make a man's three-piece suit.

 Farmers milk sheep just like cows. A sheep's milk is used to make exotic cheeses.

 An average dairy cow produces about 100 glasses of milk a day.

 The milk produced each day by a dairy cow can make 2.6 pounds of butter, 6 pounds of cheese, or 7 gallons of milk.

 Soybeans are now being used to make some crayons. They make brighter colors and are safer for children to use.

 Cows, goats, and sheep have four stomachs each. The first stomach stores the food when it is first swallowed. The animals spit up the food, chew it again, and swallow it a second time. The second stomach stores the food after it has been chewed again. The third stomach squeezes the extra water out. The last stomach digests the food.

 A cow needs about 35 gallons of water and 55 pounds of solid food (grains and hay) each day.

 One bushel of corn can sweeten about 400 cans of soda.

 There are about 600 kernels on each ear of corn.

 A bushel of wheat can be used to make 73 loaves of bread or 72 pounds of tortillas.

 The average farmer grows enough food to feed about 129 people.

Unit 6, The Moo-velous Farm: Teacher Information
Three Cheers for April PreK–K, SV 9841-8

Barn and Silo

Materials

- clean, half-gallon milk or juice cartons
- paper-towel tubes
- cone cups
- red and black paint
- hay (or yellow basket grass)
- glue gun and glue
- paintbrushes
- exacto knife
- glue

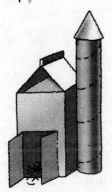

Directions

Teacher Preparation: Cut a door in the bottom of the carton. Glue the tube to the carton to look like a barn and silo.

1. Paint the carton and tube red to look like a barn and silo.
2. Paint the cone black.
3. Glue the cone on the "silo."
4. Glue hay on the barn floor.

Craft-Stick Fences

Materials

- craft sticks
- glue
- 1 cup flour
- wax paper
- ½ cup salt
- 1 cup water
- 1 tablespoon cooking oil
- 2 teaspoons cream of tartar
- resealable plastic bags
- paper plates

Directions

Teacher Preparation: Make the salt dough in advance. Each child will need about ⅓ cup of dough. In a saucepan, mix the flour, salt, water, oil, and cream of tartar. Cook the mixture over heat for three minutes, stirring occasionally. When the mixture forms a ball, remove the pan from the heat and cool it on wax paper. Knead the dough when totally cool. Store the dough in a plastic bag. Cut some craft sticks in half. Each fence section will need two craft stick halves.

1. Lay two craft sticks on a large plate so that they are about one inch apart.
2. Glue a craft stick half near each end so that the round ends reach slightly above the top stick.
3. Repeat to make three more fence sections.
4. Set the fences aside to dry.
5. Roll two small balls of dough for each fence.
6. Flatten the balls slightly.
7. Push one ball on each cut end of the craft sticks for the fence to stand on. Then let dry.

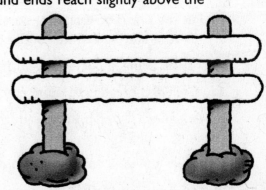

Farmer's Breakfast

You will need

- bread
- eggs
- cookie cutter in the shape of a farm animal
- cream
- salt
- craft sticks
- electric skillet with cover
- pancake turner
- small jars with lids
- cups
- cooking spray
- paper plates

Directions

Teacher Preparation: Lead children in discussing that butter comes from cows, eggs come from chickens, and bread comes from wheat. Preheat the skillet and coat it with cooking spray.

1. Fill a small jar one-quarter full of cream.

2. Add a pinch of salt to the cream.

3. Put the lid on the jar and shake the mixture to make butter.

4. Use a craft stick to spread the butter on both sides of a slice of bread.

5. Put the bread on a plate and use the cookie cutter to cut out the animal from the center. (Eat the buttered center of the bread that you cut out.)

6. Ask an adult to put what remains of the bread slice in the hot skillet to toast.

7. While the bread is toasting, crack an egg into a cup.

8. Ask an adult to flip the bread to cook on the other side and pour the raw egg into the center cutout.

9. Cover the skillet and cook the egg until it is done.

Note: Be aware of children who may have food allergies.

Three Cheers for April PreK–K, SV 9841-8

🎵 I've Been Workin' on the Old Farm

(Tune: "I've Been Workin' on the Railroad")

I've been workin' on the old farm

All the live-long day.

I've been workin' on the old farm

Hearin' what those animals say.

Can't you hear the cows a mooin',

Risin' up so early in the morn?

Can't you hear the cows
a mooin',

When (child's name) claps
his/her hands!

Other verses:

Chickens cluckin'

Roosters crowin'

Sheep baain'

Horses neighin'

Pigs oinkin'

Ducks quackin'

Extension Activity

You may wish to enlarge, duplicate,
and color the animal patterns on
pages 83 and 84 so that children
can hold them as they sing.

Books Worth Mooing About

Big Red Barn
by Margaret Wise Brown (HarperCollins)

The Farmer in the Dell: A Singing Game
by Mary Maki Rae (Viking Kestrel)

The Little Scarecrow
by Margaret Wise Brown
(Dodd Mead and Company)

Mrs. Wishy-Washy
by Joy Cowley (Philomel Books)

The Pigpen Party
by Claude Belanger (McGraw-Hill)

Sheep in a Jeep
by Nancy Shaw (Houghton Mifflin)

The Springtime Rock and Roll
by Joy Cowley (Shortland Publications)

Wake Up, Big Barn
by Suzanne Tanner Chitwood (Cartwheel Books)

What a Wonderful Day to Be a Cow
by Carolyn Lesser (Dragonfly)

Who's in the Shed?
by Brenda Parkes (Mimosa)

Three Cheers for April PreK–K, SV 9841-8

What a Moo-velous Farm!

Materials

- activity master on page 79
- pattern on page 83
- white craft paper
- overhead projector
- transparency
- tempera paints
- white construction paper
- border
- sponge brushes
- pencils
- scissors
- glue
- stapler

Directions

Teacher Preparation: Make a transparency of a completed barn using the activity master. Enlarge a copy of the cow pattern so that it fills a sheet of construction paper. Then make a copy for each child. Cover the board with the craft paper. Use the transparency to trace a large barn in the center of the bulletin board. Paint the barn and add grass along the base of the bulletin board. Add a festive border and the caption.

1. Trace one hand.

2. Cut out the hand to be an udder for the cow.

3. Cut out a cow.

4. Use a sponge brush to paint brown spots on the cow.

5. Glue the hand to the cow with the fingers pointing down.

Help children staple their cows to the bulletin board.

Barnyard Centers

Writing Center

Language Arts Standard
Uses letters to represent words

Old MacDonald's Mixed Up Farm

Materials

- patterns on pages 83 and 84
- white construction paper
- white copy paper
- scissors
- glue
- crayons

Teacher Preparation: Duplicate multiple copies of the patterns on copy paper. Then cut each animal apart to separate the head, body, and legs.

Tell children that Old MacDonald has some new animals on his farm. Then have them create new animals by choosing a head, body, and feet from different animals. Ask children to glue the pieces on construction paper and color the animal. Then have them write or dictate the animal's name and a sentence about it.

Math Center

Math Standard
Compares and recognizes *more than* and *less than* relationships

Pigpen Play

Materials

- patterns on page 80
- crayons or markers
- white construction paper
- glue
- number cube
- scissors
- file folders

Teacher Preparation: Duplicate at least two copies of the pigpen and several pigs patterns. Then color and cut out the pigpens and pigs. Glue one pigpen on each side of the inside of a file folder.

Working in pairs, children choose one side of the game board as their pigpen. Then they take turns rolling the number cube. Each child counts the number of pigs shown on the cube and places the pigs in his or her pigpen. Children compare the numbers to see who has more and who has less.

Barnyard Centers

Sensory Center

Science Standard
Understands organisms
and their environments

"Hay" There, Animals!

Materials

- tub
- hay
- plastic farm animals that eat hay

Teacher Preparation: Fill the tub with the hay.

Remind children that many farm animals eat hay. Then have children review
the animal names of the plastic farm animals you have provided. Invite one
child to hide one of the animals while the others turn away. Once the
center members face the tub, children guess the missing animal. The correct
guesser searches for the animal in the tub and pulls it out. That child then
becomes the one who hides an animal.

Science Center

Science Standard
Understands steps in
a process

Foods from the Farm

Materials

- activity master on page 81
- crayons
- glue
- sentence strips
- scissors

Teacher Preparation: Duplicate the activity master.

Explain that many foods produced on the farm change before we eat them.
Have children color the pictures and cut them apart. Then have them glue
the pictures in order on a sentence strip to show how ice cream is made,
beginning with hay. Ask children to draw a picture to show the last step—
children eating ice cream.

Barnyard Centers

Block Center

Working Farm

Materials

- plastic farm animals
- toy tractors
- barns (completed in "Barn and Silo" on page 71)
- fences (completed in "Craft-Stick Fences" on page 71)

Invite children to set up farms and pretend to be farmers. Have them place the animals in the appropriate parts of the farm. Then encourage them to complete all the farm chores that need to be done each day, from feeding the animals to working in the fields.

Art Center

Baa, Baa, Woolly Sheep

Materials

- patterns on page 82
- large paper plates
- black construction paper
- scissors
- tag board
- cotton balls
- white crayons
- glue

Teacher Preparation: Trace several patterns on tag board and cut them out for patterns. Provide two ears, two eyes, and one nose pattern for each child.

Have each child use a white crayon and the patterns to trace and cut out two ears, two eyes, and one nose from black paper for a sheep. Then have them glue cotton balls on a plate to cover the entire surface. Next, children add the ears, nose, and mouth. Have children use the white crayon to add details to the eyes of the sheep.

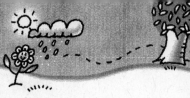

Barnyard Centers

Language Center

Language Arts Standard
Knows the alphabetical order of letters

A Farm Connection

Materials

- activity master on page 79
- crayons

Teacher Preparation: Duplicate the activity master.

Have children connect the dots from A to Z. Then invite them to color the page.

Dramatic Play Center

Social Studies Standard
Understands the importance of jobs

Farm Work

Materials

- patterns on page 82
- latex glove
- rubber bands
- black construction paper
- hot glue gun and glue
- dried ears of corn
- paintbrush
- sawhorse
- poster board
- giant spring clips
- buckets
- scissors
- overalls
- tape
- clean milk jug
- tempera paints
- cotton balls
- pin
- tub
- bandanas

Teacher Preparation: To make a cow with an udder, draw a cow outline on poster board that is big enough to cover the sawhorse. Paint it to look like a cow and tape it over the sawhorse. Fill the glove with thinned white paint and tightly rubber band the glove closed to make a cow's udder. Prick each finger of the glove. Use the giant spring clip to attach the glove to the sawhorse. To make a sheep, glue cotton balls all over the milk jug. Trace and cut out the sheep face pieces from black paper and glue them to the jug. You may wish to make several sheep.

Set the cow and sheep in the center. Place a bucket on the floor under the cow's "udder" to catch the "milk." Put the corn in the tub. Invite children to dress as farmers as they milk the cow, shear the sheep, and remove the kernels from the corn.

Name _____

ABC Farm Fun

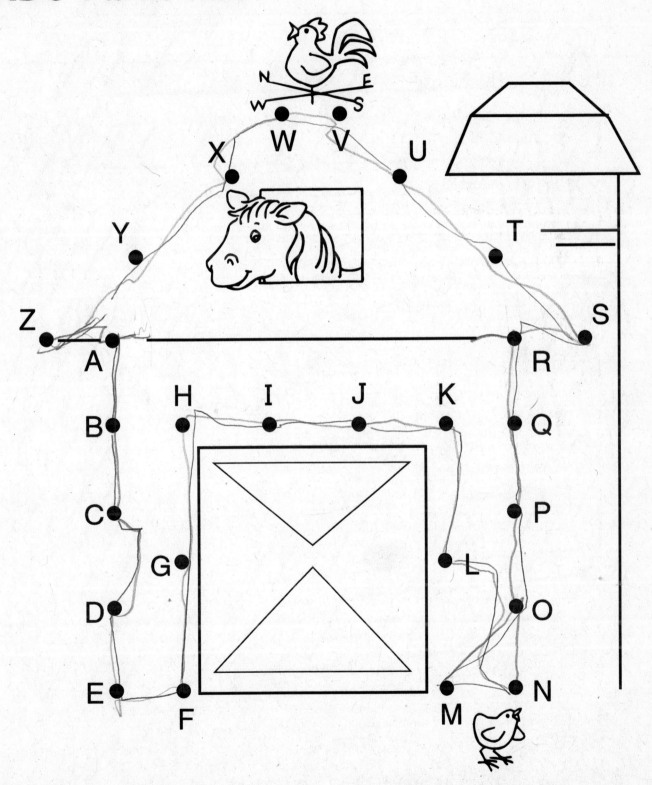

Directions: Use with "What a Moo-velous Farm!" on page 74 and "A Farm Connection" on page 78. Have children connect the dots from A to Z. Then invite them to color the page.

www.harcourtschoolsupply.com

79

Unit 6, The Moo-velous Farm: Activity Master
Three Cheers for April PreK–K, SV 9841-8

Pigpen and Pigs Patterns

Use with "Pigpen Play" on page 75.

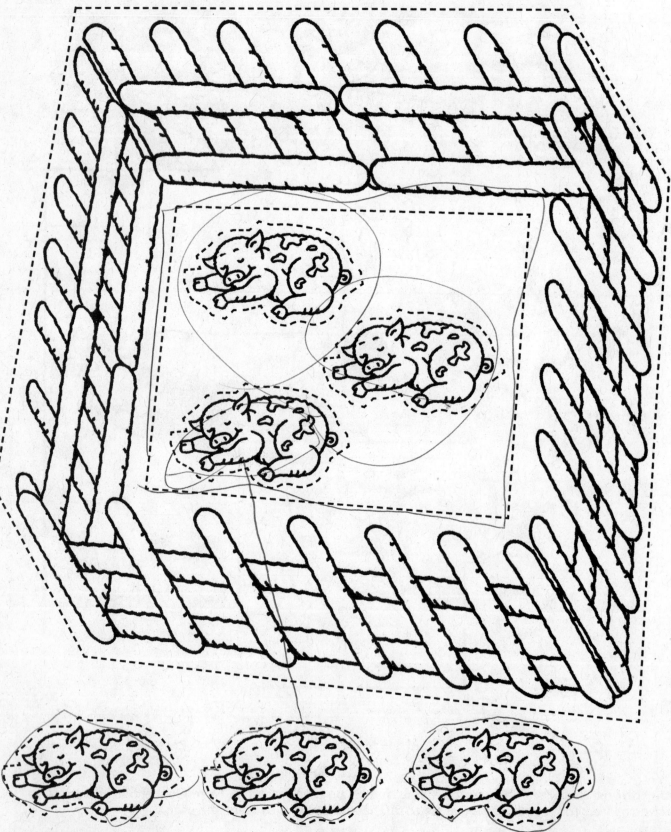

Unit 6, The Moo-velous Farm: Patterns
Three Cheers for April PreK–K, SV 9841-8

Name _____

From Farm to You

store

hay

ice cream

cow

you too

milk

Directions: Use with "Foods from the Farm" on page 76. Have children color the pictures and cut them apart. Then have them glue the pictures in order on a sentence strip to show how ice cream is made, beginning with hay. Ask children to draw a picture to show the last step—children eating ice cream.

Unit 6, The Moo-velous Farm: Activity Master
Three Cheers for April PreK–K, SV 9841-8

Sheep Face Patterns

Use with "Baa, Baa, Woolly Sheep" on page 77 and "Farm Work" on page 78.

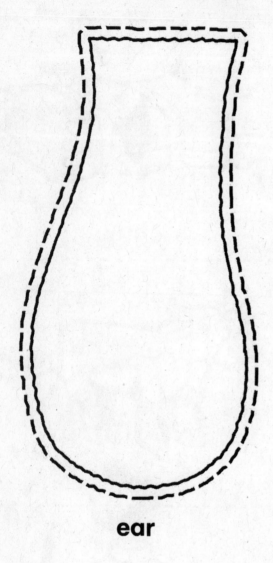

ear

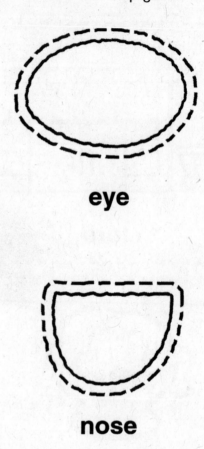

eye

nose

Three Cheers for April PreK–K, SV 9841-8

Farm Animals Patterns

Use with "What a Moo-velous Farm!" on page 74 and "Old MacDonald's Mixed Up Farm" on page 75.

cow

sheep

chicken

rooster

Three Cheers for April PreK–K, SV 9841-8

Farm Animals Patterns

Use with "Old MacDonald's Mixed Up Farm" on page 75.

goat

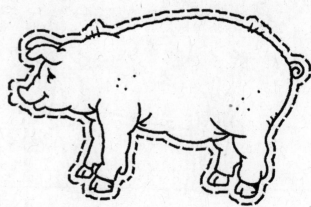

pig

horse

duck

84

Unit 6, The Moo-velous Farm: Patterns
Three Cheers for April PreK–K, SV 9841-8

A Look at John Burningham

 John Burningham, a well-known children's author and illustrator, was born April 27, 1936, in England.

 John's earliest schooling was unconventional in that he was not required to do lessons unless he wanted to. He spent many hours in the art room because that was what he wanted to do.

John did attend a formal art school in England. His first job was making puppets for a film company in Israel. On his return to England, he drew posters, cartoons, and Christmas cards.

 John is married to Helen Oxenbury, another well-known illustrator. They have three children.

 John's first book, *Borka: The Adventures of a Goose with No Feathers*, won the Kate Greenaway Medal in 1963.

 John uses a wide variety of artistic mediums, including pastels, charcoal, ink, crayons, and gouache, to give his pictures texture.

 He has won numerous awards, including the Kate Greenaway Medal twice, the New York Times Best Illustrated Book three times, and the Parent's Choice Award.

 He compares drawing to playing the piano because it is something that takes continuous practice in order to be successful.

 When John writes, he tries to capture the mental age of a five year old. Consequently, his writing uses much imagination and adventure. Even the more serious topics are wrapped in humor.

 He also illustrated the well-loved juvenile books *Chitty, Chitty Bang Bang: The Magical Car* by Ian Fleming and *The Wind in the Willows* by Kenneth Graham.

 John also creates large murals, wall friezes, magazine illustrations, and advertisements.

Mr. Gumpy's Motor Car
by John Burningham

Display the cover of *Mr. Gumpy's Motor Car* and help children identify the animals they see. Challenge them to predict where the car is going and what might happen.

Retell the Story
Materials

- patterns on pages 89 and 90
- white and red construction paper
- crayons
- scissors

Directions

Teacher Preparation: Duplicate the car pattern on red construction paper and the character patterns on white construction paper.

Ask children to cut out the car. Then have them color and cut out the characters. Invite children to retell *Mr. Gumpy's Motor Car* using their props.

Real or Make-Believe
Materials

- activity master on page 91
- crayons

Directions

Teacher Preparation: Duplicate the activity master.

Lead children in a discussion of parts of the book that could really happen and those that could not. Then have children color the picture in each row that shows something that could really happen.

Books by John Burningham

- *Avocado Baby* (Red Fox)

- *Borka: The Adventures of a Goose with No Feathers* (Random House UK Distribution)

This book may be used with the Eggs-actly Eggs unit.

- *Cloudland* (Knopf Books for Young Readers)

- *Come Away from the Water, Shirley* (Crowell)

- *Granpa* (Red Fox)

- *Hey! Get Off Our Train* (Dragonfly)

This book may be used with the Our Earth unit.

- *Husherbye* (Knopf Books for Young Readers)

- *John Burningham's ABC* (Random House)

- *The Magic Bed* (Knopf Books for Young Readers)

- *Mr. Gumpy's Outing* (Henry Holt & Company)

- *Numbers* (Candlewick Press)

- *Pigs Plus* (Walker Books)

This book may be used with the Moo-velous Farm unit.

- *Where's Julius?* (Red Fox)

- *Would You Rather?* (SeaStar Books)

Bookmark Patterns

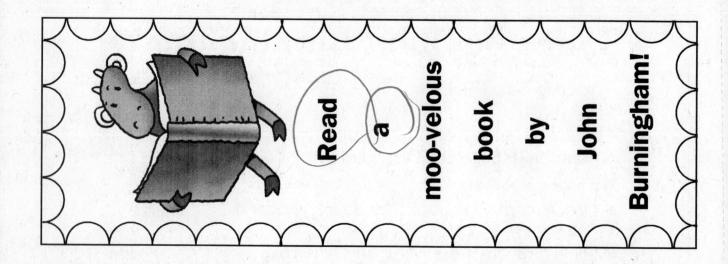

Read a moo-velous book by John Burningham!

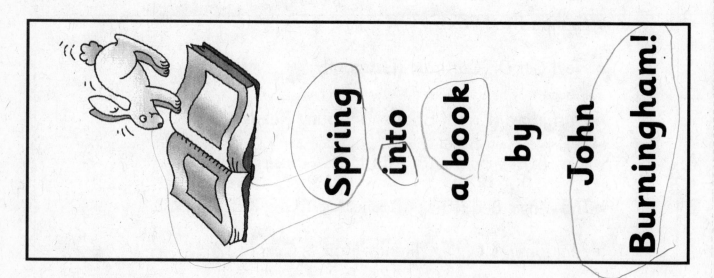

Spring into a book by John Burningham!

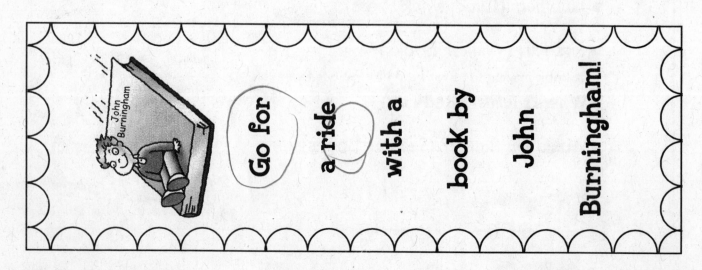

Go for a ride with a book by John Burningham!

Unit 7, Author Study: Patterns

Three Cheers for April PreK–K, SV 9841-8

Real or Make-Believe

Directions: Use with "Real or Make-Believe" on page 86. Have children color the picture in each row that shows something that could really happen.

Center Icons Patterns

Art Center

Block Center

Dramatic Play Center

Game Center

Three Cheers for April PreK–K, SV 9841-8

Center Icons Patterns

Language Center

Math Center

Music Center

Puzzle Center

Three Cheers for April PreK–K, SV 9841-8

Center Icons Patterns

Reading Center

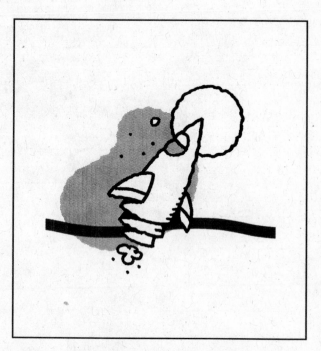

Science Center

Sensory Center

Writing Center

94

Center Icons Patterns
Three Cheers for April PreK–K, SV 9841-8

Student Awards

You are doing eggs-tremely well in

_____

_____

_____

_____

Child's name

_____

Teacher's signature　　　　　**Date**

_____

_____

Child's name

Congratulations,

**You are the April
Student of the Month for**

_____

_____

_____

Teacher's signature　　　　　**Date**

Student Awards Patterns
Three Cheers for April PreK–K, SV 9841-8

Student Award

How moo-velous!

_____

-     can   I LOve You lik you

_____

Teacher's signature   **Date**

Calendar Day Pattern

Suggested Uses

- Reproduce one card for each day of the month. Write the numerals on each card and place it on your class calendar. Use cards to mark special days.
- Reproduce to make cards to use in word ladders or word walls.
- Reproduce to make cards and write a letter on each card. Children use the cards to form words.
- Reproduce to make cards to create matching or concentration games for students to use in activity centers. Choose from the following possible matching skills or create your own:
  — uppercase and lowercase letters
  — pictures of objects whose names rhyme, have the same beginning or ending sounds, contain short or long vowels
  — pictures of adult animals and baby animals
  — numerals and pictures of objects
  — number words and numerals
  — colors and shapes
  — high-frequency sight words

Three Cheers for April PreK–K, SV 9841-8